THIS
OR THAT...
OR THAT?
QUIZ
BOOK

by Emma MacLaren Henke
illustrated by Zoe Persico

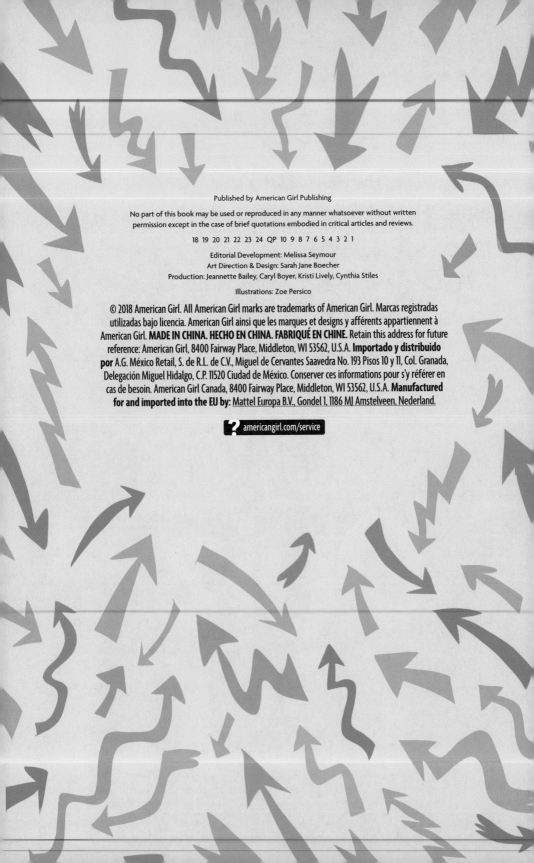

Published by American Girl Publishing

18 19 20 21 22 23 24 QP 10 9 8 7 6 5 4 3 2 1

Editorial Development: Melissa Seymour
Art Direction & Design: Sarah Jane Boecher
Production: Jeannette Bailey, Caryl Boyer, Kristi Lively, Cynthia Stiles

Illustrations: Zoe Persico

americangirl.com/service

DEAR READER,

Do you like to keep your options open? Whether you're looking for fun **OR** insight **OR** a few laughs, this is the book for you.

Answer the questions inside to discover more about yourself **OR** your friends **OR** your family. Consider your favorites **OR** your fears **OR** your fantasies. Find out how you see yourself **OR** your future **OR** your world. Pick what makes you laugh **OR** cry **OR** cringe. This book has more than 500 chances to choose and let you weigh all the pros **AND** cons **AND** in-betweens!

No matter how you decide to use this book—at a party **OR** on a road trip **OR** to pass the time on a rainy day—you're sure to find it filled with fun. So sit down by yourself **OR** with a pal **OR** with your whole gang for some dandy decisions. Just grab a pencil **OR** a pen **OR** a marker and turn the page!

YOUR FRIENDS AT AMERICAN GIRL

TABLE OF CONTENTS

COMPETITIVE SPIRIT

It's not whether you win or lose, it's how you play the game that counts! Answer these quick questions to see what kind of player you are.

Playing video games with your younger cousin, would you . . .

share your best moves

OR

let her win

OR

compete your hardest?

Do you prefer to compete . . .

with a team, like in soccer

OR

on your own, like in a spelling bee

OR

on your own and for a team at the same time, like at a swim meet?

If you had a chance to sink the game-winning basket, would you feel . . .

calm and confident **OR**

shaky and sweaty

OR

happy and hopeful?

When you win a close game, are you the first to . . .

cheer on your team-mates for their victory

OR

point out the tough plays you made

OR

congratulate the other team for its great effort?

HAVE YOU EVER?

Gather your pals to find out who's done what. Each person raises her hand when she can answer "Yes!"

Have you ever...

traveled outside your state **OR** to another country **OR** to another continent?

run a mile **OR** hiked 10 miles **OR** biked 50 miles?

found a wallet **OR** a lost dog **OR** a four-leaf clover?

worn your hair in a French braid **OR** a French twist **OR** a fishtail braid?

failed a test **OR** gotten a detention **OR** been grounded?

forgotten your lunch **OR** your homework **OR** your backpack?

crochet?

learned to knit **OR** sew **OR**

JUST ONE THING

If you could, how would you change the people you know?

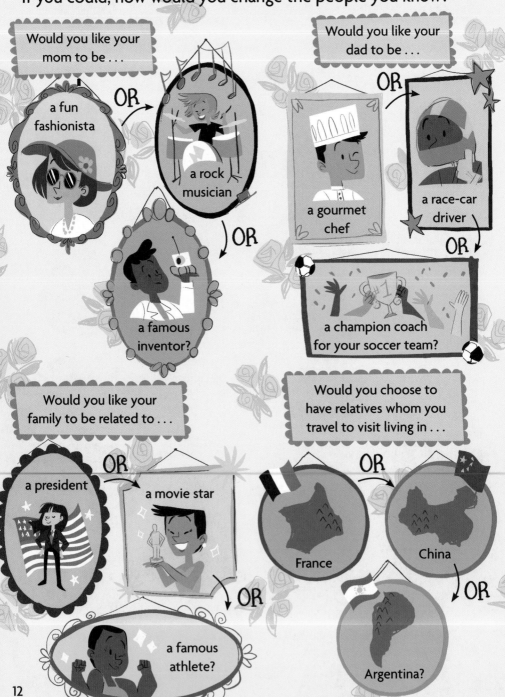

Would you like your mom to be . . .

a fun fashionista

OR

a rock musician

OR

a famous inventor?

Would you like your dad to be . . .

a gourmet chef

OR

a race-car driver

OR

a champion coach for your soccer team?

Would you like your family to be related to . . .

a president

OR

a movie star

OR

a famous athlete?

Would you choose to have relatives whom you travel to visit living in . . .

France

OR

China

OR

Argentina?

TRUTH OR TRUTH OR TRUTH?

Do you dare? Play this version of the classic party game by taking turns with friends choosing which truth to tell.

Share your biggest hope

OR

biggest worry

OR

biggest fantasy.

Give details about your quirkiest habit

OR

your most embarrassing habit

OR

a habit you'd like to break.

Talk about the last fight you had with a friend

OR

a sibling

OR

your mom.

Say whether you believe that some people can read minds

OR

see the future

OR

move objects with their minds.

Share the worst grade you ever got

OR

the worst punishment you ever got

OR

the worst injury you've had.

Talk about the best gift you've ever given

OR

the best gift you've ever received

OR

the gift you most want.

Describe the most embarrassing thing that's ever happened to you at school

OR

with your family

OR

in front of a large group of people.

Describe the inside of your locker

OR

the inside of your closet

OR

the inside of your desk at school.

Share your nickname as a baby

OR

your grandma's pet name for you

OR

the name your siblings call you when they're teasing you.

Say whether you believe in ghosts

OR

aliens

OR

vampires.

Tell the strangest food you've ever eaten

OR

the messiest food you've ever eaten

OR

the food you eat when no one is looking.

Describe your dream job

OR

the job you think you'll have

OR

a job you'd hate to have.

Tell your biggest fear involving school

OR

your friends

OR

your family.

Describe one way you're jealous of your best friend

OR

your sibling

OR

your classmate.

Describe one thing you'd change about your style

OR

how you handle school

OR

how you treat people.

Say whether you believe in love at first sight

OR

that opposites attract

OR

that all's fair in love and war.

GROUP DYNAMICS

Do you like to spend time all alone OR with one best friend OR with the whole gang? Take this quiz with your pals, and then compare answers!

Would you rather . . .

go to the movies . . .

all alone OR with one best friend OR with the whole gang?

work on a science fair project . . .

all alone OR with one best friend OR with the whole gang?

get dressed up for the school dance . . .

all alone OR with one best friend OR with the whole gang?

go sledding . . .

all alone OR with one best friend OR with the whole gang?

volunteer for your favorite good cause . . .

all alone OR with one best friend OR with the whole gang?

plan your school's talent show . . .

all alone OR with one best friend OR with the whole gang?

get lost in the woods . . .

all alone OR with one best friend OR with the whole gang?

go to a dance class . . .

all alone OR with one best friend OR with the whole gang?

make a music video . . .

all alone OR with one best friend OR with the whole gang?

try out new hairstyles . . .

all alone OR with one best friend OR with the whole gang?

go horseback riding . . .

all alone OR with one best friend OR with the whole gang?

take an archery class . . .

all alone OR with one best friend OR with the whole gang?

camp overnight in your backyard . . .

all alone OR with one best friend OR with the whole gang?

learn to bake homemade bread . . .

all alone OR with one best friend OR with the whole gang?

try out for your school play . . .

all alone OR with one best friend OR with the whole gang?

spend an hour in detention . . .

all alone OR with one best friend OR with the whole gang?

spend the last day of summer vacation . . .

all alone OR with one best friend OR with the whole gang?

FLOWER POWER

Which posy would you pick?

In the past, people gave bouquets to send secret messages. Different flowers conveyed different ideas. Take a look at the flowers and meanings below; then choose which flowers you'd share in each situation.

sunflower
{ADORATION}

tulip
{FAME}

daffodil
{RESPECT AND REGARD}

daisy
{INNOCENCE}

violet
{MODESTY}

orchid
{LUXURY AND REFINED BEAUTY}

red rose
{LOVE}

yellow rose
{FRIENDSHIP}

fern
{FASCINATION}

lilac
{YOUTHFUL SPIRIT}

Turn the page and use
your flower knowledge!

19

You'd give your mom a Mother's Day bouquet of . . .

red roses OR lilacs OR orchids.

Your best friend should wear a . . .

sunflower OR daffodil OR daisy.

You'd bring your teacher a vase of . . .

daffodils OR tulips OR yellow roses.

You'd grow your dad a gift of . . .

sunflowers OR ferns OR daffodils.

You'd bring your big sister a graduation bouquet made from . . .

lilacs OR daffodils OR yellow roses.

You'd decorate your room with a vase of . . .

violets OR orchids OR lilacs.

You'd toss your favorite celebrity a bunch of . . .

daffodils OR orchids OR sunflowers.

You'd celebrate your friend's starring role in the school play with a gift of . . .

tulips OR yellow roses OR sunflowers.

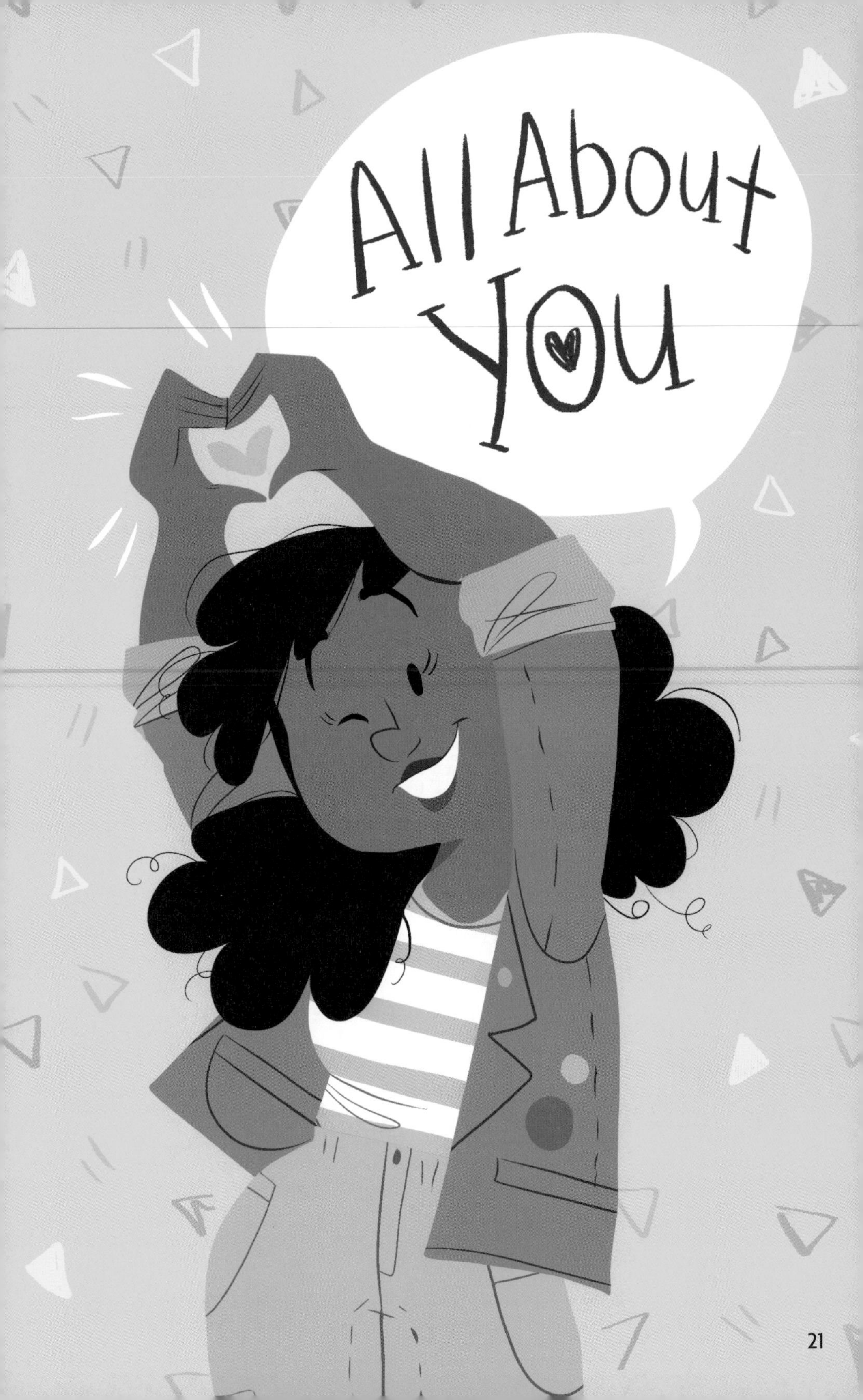
All About You

CHOOSY CHEF

When you're in charge in the kitchen, would your menu include . . .

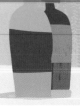

ranch dressing

OR

French dressing

OR

Italian dressing?

an iceberg lettuce wedge

OR

a spinach salad

OR

mixed raw veggies?

chocolate mousse

OR

lemon mousse

OR

smoked salmon mousse?

macaroni

OR

spaghetti

OR

butterfly pasta?

biscuits

OR

a baguette

OR

bagels?

a berry bowl

OR

mixed melon chunks

OR

a citrus salad?

sprinkles

OR

frosting

OR

powdered sugar?

buffalo wings

OR

teriyaki wings

OR

honey mustard wings?

cake

OR

cookies

OR

pie?

shrimp

OR

lobster

OR

crab?

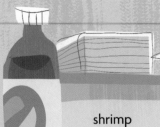

cheese pizza
OR
cheese puffs
OR
macaroni and cheese?

orange juice
OR
apple juice
OR
grape juice?

fish fry
OR
fish sticks
OR
sushi?

pork chops
OR
pork roast
OR
bacon?

EGGS

meatless Monday
OR
taco Tuesday
OR
fish Friday?

alfredo
OR
marinara
OR
pesto?

yogurt

milk shakes
OR
smoothies
OR
frozen lemonade?

BUTTER

MILK

eating leftovers for breakfast
OR
lunch
OR
dinner?

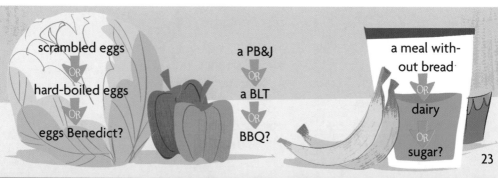

scrambled eggs
OR
hard-boiled eggs
OR
eggs Benedict?

a PB&J
OR
a BLT
OR
BBQ?

a meal without bread
OR
dairy
OR
sugar?

23

LEADER OF THE PACK

What kind of leader are you? What kind of leader do you like to follow?

Would you rather...

be a governor
OR
a mayor
OR
a sheriff?

plan a party
OR
a trip
OR
a school group project?

conduct an orchestra
OR
direct a play
OR
film a movie?

be a movie writer
OR
a movie director
OR
a movie costume designer?

pilot a passenger jet
OR
a steamboat
OR
a space mission?

be your own boss at a tech company
OR
a fashion design studio
OR
a restaurant?

teach your best friend a recipe by writing out instructions
OR
by making the recipe with her
OR
by having her cook the recipe and then tasting the results?

run for student council representative
OR
student council treasurer
OR
student council president?

create classroom rules
OR
enforce classroom rules
OR
follow classroom rules?

be captain of the
basketball team
OR
the dance team
OR
the debate team?

have a
teacher who's
strict but fair
OR
loose and
laid-back
OR
bossy but
funny?

teach your friends a new
board game by reading
the rules out loud
OR
by playing a
practice round
OR
by using new players'
mistakes to your
advantage?

show a new student
the rules at school by
writing a list of what to
do and what not to do
OR
loudly pointing out when a
student breaks the rules
OR
following the rules yourself
to set a good example?

live in a country
ruled by a good
and kind queen
OR
a panel of the
smartest citizens
OR
leaders elected by
the people?

be a camp
counselor
OR
a camp
director
OR
just go
camping on
your own?

navigate for
a group hike
with a map
OR
with the GPS
on your phone
OR
using the signs
of nature?

make the
rules yourself
OR
vote on the rules
with a group
OR
forget about
following rules?

lead a mountain-
biking tour
OR
a city
street-food tour
OR
a tour of your
school for a
new student?

IT'S BETTER TO GIVE

Do you have a gift for choosing perfect presents? Select surprises for everyone in your life!

Would you choose to...

give your best bud a present of . . .

homemade cupcakes

OR

a beautifully braided bracelet

OR

a picture you painted yourself?

give a classmate a gift of . . .

colored gel pens

OR

locker magnets

OR

chocolate?

give your favorite teammate . . .

a hand-decorated water bottle

OR

a gift certificate for a sports massage

OR

a jersey with her favorite athlete's name?

give your teacher . . .

a fruit basket

OR

a gift card to his favorite bookstore

OR a funny coffee mug?

give your mom a birthday gift of . . .

a bouquet of flowers you grew

OR a pretty cake you made yourself

OR a cap you crocheted?

give your little brother . . .

a water-balloon slingshot

OR

a new sketchbook

OR trading cards for his favorite sports team?

give your parents an anniversary gift of . . .

a romantic dinner for two cooked by you

OR

an at-home movie night, with you providing popcorn and a flick they pick

OR

a special family recipe book filled with all their favorites?

give your guests a party favor of . . .

friendship bracelets

OR homemade chocolate truffles

OR funny photo frames?

give your neighbor . . .

a coupon for your free services as a weed puller

OR

plant waterer

OR

lawn mower?

bring a baby shower gift of . . .

a baby blanket you knit yourself

OR

a copy of your favorite picture book

OR

a coupon for free babysitting by you?

give your big sister . . .

tickets to see her favorite band

OR

tickets to a video game conference

OR

tickets to an amusement park?

give your favorite cousin a wedding gift of . . .

kitchen towels with your own hand-embroidered designs

OR

personalized stationery for the married couple

OR

a coupon for pet sitting by you while the couple is on their honeymoon?

give your grandparents . . .

a special photo of you and your siblings together

OR

a special family dinner cooked by all their grandchildren

OR

a hand-picked playlist filled with your favorite music and theirs?

bring a party hostess a gift of . . .

homemade peanut brittle

OR

a potholder made by you

OR

a six-pack of your favorite special soda?

27

SPA DAY!

How would you prefer to be pampered?

Would you rather...

take a class in yoga

OR

meditation

OR

tai chi?

decorate your fingernails with rainbow colors

OR

sparkle polish

OR

a French manicure?

treat your skin with a honey-banana face mask

OR

a cucumber eye mask

OR

an oatmeal body scrub?

sip sparkling water

OR

sparkling cider

OR

a strawberry spritzer?

get a hot stone massage

OR

an aromatherapy massage

OR

a deep tissue massage?

ask your best friend to cut your hair

OR

paint your toenails

OR

choose your outfits for a month?

give your mom a back rub

OR

pedicure

OR

hand massage?

go to school wearing a spa robe and slippers

OR

a mud mask

OR

too much perfume?

get cozy with hot cocoa

OR

hot tea

OR

warm milk?

give yourself a manicure

OR

a pedicure

OR

both?

visit the spa with your best friend

OR

your mom

OR

your favorite celebrity?

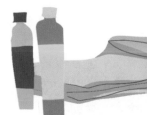

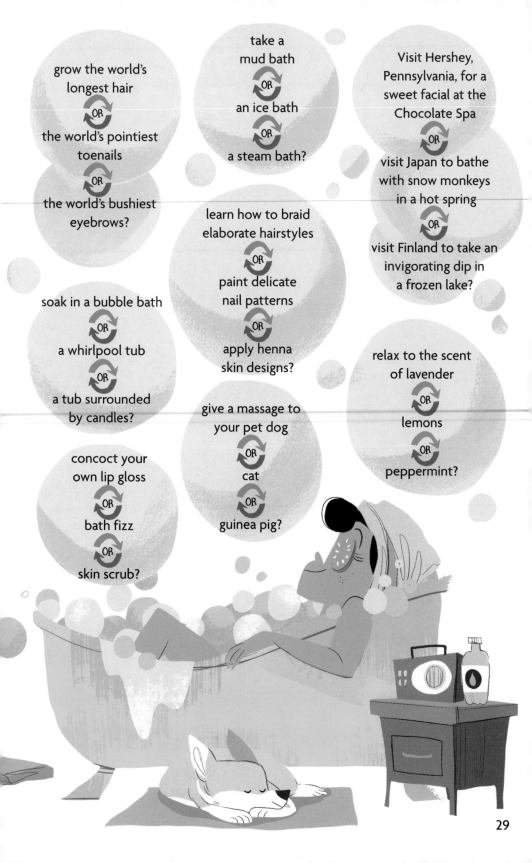

NO RISK, NO REWARD

What's your tolerance for taking a chance?

Would you rather...

walk a
paved path

OR

hike a
state park

OR

climb a
mountain?

dance in your room
to your favorite tunes

OR

at a party with
your friends

OR

onstage in
a recital?

play
solitaire

OR

charades

OR

truth or dare?

ride a bike

OR

a skateboard

OR

a unicycle?

go to summer
day camp

OR

a sleep-away
camp an
hour from
your home

OR

a wilderness
camp halfway
across the
country?

try a meal of
a pork chop
and potatoes

OR

spicy
buffalo wings

OR

sea urchin sushi?

count the
votes for
your class
election

OR

run for class
secretary

OR

run for class
president?

shoot a layup

OR

a free throw

OR

a three-point shot?

jump in
feet first
OR
do a
cannonball
OR
do a flip?

work with animals
in a pet store
OR
at a zoo
OR
in the
wild?

jump
through a
game of
hopscotch
OR
across a
narrow creek
OR
off the 10-meter
high dive?

try gymnastics
on the floor mat
OR
on the
balance beam
OR
on the
uneven bars?

try
out for
a school
play
OR
a play at a local
theater
OR
a Broadway show?

travel by yourself to
your grandma's house
OR
to visit a friend
in another state
OR
into space on
a rocket ship?

compete in your
school science fair
OR
the all-city
science fair
OR
the national
science fair?

sign up for
karate lessons
OR
rock-climbing
lessons
OR
trapeze lessons?

wear a
swim-team
bathing suit
OR
a cute
halter suit
OR
a surfing wetsuit?

NATURE MADE

Choose your outdoor adventure!

Would you rather...

get lost in the woods **OR** the mountains **OR** a city park?

sleep in a camper **OR** in a tent **OR** right under the stars?

try to build a fire with no matches **OR** build a shelter with no tarp **OR** catch a fish with no hook?

take a ride behind a team of sled dogs **OR** in a hot-air balloon **OR** on a zip line?

bug juice? **OR** chili

invent your own recipe for specialty s'mores **OR**

paddle a canoe with a soup spoon **OR** ride a raft made of ice pop sticks **OR** sail a boat using a beach towel to catch the wind?

volunteer at a state park to help clear trails **OR** classify plants **OR** lead a nature hike?

forage for mushrooms OR catch a fish OR pick wild berries?

plant a vegetable garden OR an herb garden OR a flower garden?

swim fins? OR tap shoes OR climb a mountain wearing high heels

explore an underground crystal cave OR a plunging rain-forest waterfall OR a tropical coral reef?

navigate your way using the stars OR a compass OR the shapes of trees?

at a bustling city seashore OR catch some rays on a deserted Caribbean beach OR by your own backyard swimming pool?

the wide-open prairie? OR the mountains OR watch the sun set over the ocean

work as a park ranger OR a sheep rancher OR a marine biologist?

33

DEAR DIARY

How would you finish these journal prompts?

I'm happiest when I'm . . .

at home **OR** at school

OR

out with my friends.

I love to talk about . . .

my family **OR** my friends **OR** my adventures.

I feel confused when I . . .

get a bad grade **OR** get mad at my friends **OR** get in trouble at home.

I love it when my friends . . .

share secrets with me **OR** spend time with me **OR** make me laugh.

I wish I was better at controlling . . .

my temper **OR** my nerves **OR** my bad habits.

When I feel happy, I . . .

like to be around other people **OR** do my best work at school and on projects

When I feel sad, I like to . . .

spend time alone **OR** spend time with friends and family **OR** spend time doing a fun activity. **OR** smile!

I wish my friends knew . . .

how much I care for them OR that they can always count on me OR how grateful I am to them.

One thing I'm looking forward to about growing up is . . .

learning to drive OR going to college OR getting my dream job.

To me, a ray of sunshine is like . . .

a warm smile OR an alarm clock telling me to make the most of the day OR a warning to put on some sunscreen!

Sometimes when I daydream, I'm thinking about . . .

my ideal job OR my ideal vacation OR my ideal day.

WOOF WOOF!

I think pets are . . .

nice for some people but not for me OR lots of fun, and a great way to learn responsibility OR the best friends you can have.

My ideal day would include . . .

the best outfit ever OR travel to an exotic location OR time with my friends.

Walking barefoot in the grass makes me feel . . .

appreciation for the beauty of nature OR hopeful for the future OR too cold!

If I ever became rich and famous, I'd like to . . .

take care of all my friends and family OR use the spotlight to spread the word about causes that are important to me. OR live a life of luxury!

Don't Forget!!!
· water plants
· clean room
· walk dog

35

SOCIAL STYLE

Are you an introvert, an extrovert, or somewhere in between?

Would you prefer to...

be the life of the party
OR
a wallflower
OR
a party crasher?

star in the school play
OR
play a part in the chorus
OR
help with costumes backstage?

host a study session
OR
be part of a study group
OR
borrow notes from your best bud?

hear a joke
OR
tell a joke
OR
do a stand-up comedy routine?

spend the weekend at a multitroop scout campout
OR
at the library, curled up with a good book
OR
at home, where you can spend some time on your own and some with your family?

keep a conversation going, no matter what
OR
speak up when you've got something interesting to say
OR
mostly just listen?

HA HA HA!

zzZZ

play a solo recital

OR

play in a band

OR

clap along in the audience?

work as a chef leading a busy restaurant kitchen

OR

as a private chef for a family

OR

as a solo recipe tester for a new cookbook?

eat breakfast with your friends at school

OR

eat breakfast at home

OR

eat breakfast in bed?

give a speech to your whole class

OR

make a presentation to your teacher, one-on-one,

OR

write a report?

take a hike with a big group of friends

OR

with one best friend

OR

just with your dog?

visit a famous beach in a big city

OR

a fun family beach resort

OR

a deserted tropical island?

meet 100 new friends in a day

OR

meet 10 new friends in a day

OR

meet one new friend in a day?

show your best friend a video of yourself singing your favorite pop song

OR

demonstrating your unique hobby

OR

reviewing your favorite book?

go to a movie alone

OR

go to a movie with a group of friends

OR

star in a movie?

send an e-mail to one friend

OR

send a group text to five friends

OR

write a piece in your school magazine?

argue your opinions until all your friends are convinced

OR

state your opinions so you know they're heard among other ideas

OR

keep your opinions to yourself?

shout out your answer in class

OR

raise your hand when you know an answer

OR

never volunteer to answer?

have every minute of your weekend filled with activities

OR

have some activities and some downtime on the weekend

OR

have no weekend commitments at all so you can do whatever you like?

celebrate your birthday at a huge surprise party thrown by your pals

OR

at your favorite restaurant with family and a few friends

OR

at home with your parents and your mom's delicious birthday cake?

TICKTOCK

Are you on top of time, or do you tend to procrastinate?

Are you more likely to...

write a book report a week before it's due **OR** the day before it's due **OR** the morning it's due?

do your homework as soon as you get home from school **OR** before you go to bed **OR** during lunch period right before class?

never hit the snooze button **OR** hit the snooze button one time, then get up **OR** hit the snooze button at least three times every morning?

be the first one at the school bus stop **OR** just make it to the bus on time **OR** miss the school bus?

pack your lunch before you go to bed the night before **OR** when you get up in the morning **OR** beg your mom for lunch money as you race out the door to school?

make valentines for your classmates before the end of January **OR** the last weekend before Valentine's Day **OR** before school on the morning of February 14?

Would you rather...

pick out what you'll wear to school a week in advance **OR** before you go to bed **OR** as you're getting dressed in the morning?

start studying for a test as soon as you know when the test will be **OR** a few days before the test **OR** a few minutes before the test?

bring home your PE clothes to be washed after every gym class **OR** once a week **OR** at the end of the school year, when you clean out your locker?

respond to e-mails and text messages as soon as you get them **OR** once or twice a day **OR** when you need a reply back right away?

check off every item on your school to-do list **OR** check off a few items on your to-do list **OR** not make a to-do list?

do your best school-work a little bit at a time, well before any deadlines **OR** near the time when it's due **OR** at the very last minute?

turn in a homework assignment before it's due **OR** on the day it's due **OR** a day late?

practice for your band recital for months **OR** for a few weeks **OR** for a few days before the show?

41

SUBJECT MATTER

Which classes pass your test to be the best?

Would you prefer to...

study ancient Rome **OR** ancient Egypt **OR** ancient China?

diagram the branches of government **OR** a rain-forest ecosystem **OR** a sentence?

draw a portrait **OR** a flag **OR** a data table?

win the science fair **OR** the spelling bee **OR** the math Olympics?

read a novel **OR** a science textbook **OR** the newspaper?

go to the lab for biology **OR** chemistry **OR** physics?

play dodgeball **OR** run a sprint **OR** learn to square dance?

skip PE **OR** music class **OR** art?

take a cooking class **OR** woodworking class **OR** robotics class?

take a pop quiz on geometry **OR** geography **OR** geology?

write a poem **OR** a report **OR** a computer program?

paint a picture in history class **OR** write a report in math class **OR** take an essay test in PE class?

learn to speak Spanish **OR** Arabic **OR** Japanese?

debate the meaning of a poem **OR** the significance of the Civil War **OR** the reasons for the demise of dinosaurs?

find out more about Labor Day **OR** Presidents' Day **OR** Earth Day?

watch a play **OR** read a play **OR** perform in a play?

catch up on studying during lunch **OR** recess **OR** your bus ride home?

take a field trip for science class **OR** art class **OR** history class?

practice printing **OR** cursive **OR** typing?

have more time for lunch **OR** study hall **OR** recess?

SWEET SUPPLIES

Which school tools are your favorites? Take your pick from each list of school loot.

Would you prefer...

pencil:

yellow #2

OR

mechanical

OR

patterned and pretty?

pens:

black only

OR

every color in the rainbow

OR

erasable?

pencil sharpener:

handheld

OR

electric

OR

hand-crank, on the wall of your classroom?

pencil case:

slim and sleek

OR

bold and stylish

OR

as large as possible?

notebook:

composition book

OR

spiral bound

OR

color coded for each class?

backpack:

animal print

OR

your favorite color

OR

rugged and ready for hiking?

eraser:

standard pink

OR

white artist's eraser

OR

shaped like your favorite cute cartoon character?

locker decor:

mirror

OR

whiteboard

OR

cute magnets?

water bottle:

stainless steel

OR

unbreakable plastic

OR

painted to match your lunch box?

crayons:
24-pack
OR
64-pack
OR
128-pack?

markers:
fine tip
OR
thick tip
OR
permanent?

lunch box:
metal
OR
soft-sided and insulated
OR
brown paper bag?

calculator:
just the basic functions
OR
solar-powered
OR
includes math tips and formulas?

gym shoes:
super stylish
OR
comfy running shoes
OR
high-tops?

calendar:
oversize wall calendar
OR
handheld day planner
OR
online calendar?

note cards:
blank white
OR
lined
OR
colored?

computer:
desktop
OR
laptop
OR
tablet?

HOMEWORK HAPPINESS

How do you handle homework best?

Would you prefer to...

work as quickly as you can
OR
review each page
as you complete it
OR
check every single answer?

write the first draft
of an essay in a
notebook
OR
on your computer
OR
on note cards, so you
can rearrange the
paragraphs?

work math problems in
your head
OR
on graph paper
OR
using a calculator?

study for a test for
10 hours straight
OR
for an hour a day
for 10 days
OR
for just 10 minutes
right before the
test?

study with your friends
OR
your parents
OR
all alone?

study for a test using
flash cards
OR
by rereading the
chapter
OR
by explaining the
material to your dad?

write homework in calligraphy
OR
crayon
OR
invisible ink?

study in your room
OR
at the library
OR
outside?

research a report
at the library
OR
using the Internet
OR
by doing interviews?

take notes
in pencil
OR
pen
OR
on your computer?

memorize math facts
OR
state capitals
OR
a poem?

have 20 minutes of
homework every night
OR
have 2 hours of
homework once a week
OR
have a huge 20-page report
and presentation as your
only homework for the
whole school year?

do a book report
on a biography
OR
a mystery
OR
a sci-fi novel?

write a short story
OR
a descriptive sketch
OR
a persuasive essay?

fill in a political map
OR
a climate map
OR
a road map?

give a speech
OR
perform a scene
from a play
OR
write a skit?

get homework help
from your parents
OR
your teacher
OR
your friends?

study spelling
OR
vocabulary—what
words mean
OR
etymology—where
words come from?

assign homework
to your teacher
OR
your parents
OR
your siblings?

BE THE TEACHER

Imagine you make the rules at school!

Would you rather...

teach at an all-girls school
OR
an all-boys school
OR
a school for girls and boys?

give out 100
detentions in a day
OR
give out 1 detention a
day for 100 days
OR
go 100 days without
giving a detention?

write out your lesson
plans in calligraphy
OR
with watercolor paints
OR
with stencil lettering?

take your class on a field
trip to a planetarium
OR
an art museum
OR
a nature preserve?

teach a class
full of robots
OR
pirates
OR
aliens?

have a classroom
with no desks
OR
no chairs
OR
no blackboard?

teach a class full of
fairy-tale characters
OR
superheroes
OR
witches and wizards?

have your class-
room inside
a mall
OR
in an igloo
OR
at the zoo?

grade essay tests

OR

multiple-choice tests

OR

oral exams?

be a lunch monitor

OR

a recess monitor

OR

a hallway monitor?

be known as the funny teacher

OR

the strict teacher

OR

the cool teacher?

hang out in a teacher's lounge stocked with cookies and milk

OR

massage chairs

OR

magazines and newspapers?

have a class filled with teacher's pets

OR

class clowns

OR

know-it-alls?

let students chew gum in class

OR

punish gum chewers by making them scrape old gum off desks

OR

make gum chewers bring gum for everyone?

reward good grades with smiley stickers

OR

extra recess

OR

nothing, since hard work is its own reward?

surprise your students with a pop quiz

OR

an outdoor class session

OR

doughnuts for everyone?

decorate your classroom with posters of nature scenes

OR

funny animals

OR

sports teams?

teach at a school for the performing arts

OR

an athletic academy

OR

a bilingual school?

assign your class to research medieval castles

OR

undersea life

OR

ancient languages?

GO TEAM!

What would you do to show school spirit or support your sport?

Would you rather ...

decorate for a school pep
rally with balloons

OR

posters

OR

disco lights?

hang a school flag
in your room

OR

on your family's car

OR

on your locker?

always wear the same
socks on game day

OR

always wear the same
underwear on game day

OR

always eat the same
lunch on game day?

set your phone ring tone
to your school's fight song

OR

set your computer color
scheme to match school colors

OR

use your school's mascot as
your online avatar?

make up a new cheer

OR

choreograph a dance
routine for a pep rally

OR

make your own pom-poms?

bake cookies to share
with your teammates

OR

make good luck charms to
share with your teammates

OR

write encouraging notes for
your teammates?

lead a cheer at
a pep rally

OR

perform a dance
at a pep rally

OR

sit in a dunk tank
at a pep rally?

wear your team uniform for games only

OR

all day on game days

OR

every day of the year?

do the splits

OR

do a flip

OR

be part of a human pyramid?

be a member of the pep band

OR

the cheerleading squad

OR

the team on the field?

write about your team for the school paper

OR

post photos of your team on the school's website

OR

record videos of your team's games and share them on your school website?

sing the school song with the crowd

OR

sing the national anthem for the crowd

OR

sing "We Are the Champions" after a big win?

paint your nails school colors

OR

paint your face school colors

OR

paint your room school colors?

cheer on your team with a pom-pom

OR

a cow bell

OR

a megaphone?

raise money for
your team by selling
game-time snacks

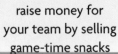 OR

by selling handmade
team pennants

OR

by organizing a
team car wash?

design a new
school mascot

OR

write a new
school song

OR

paint a giant school
spirit mural on
your gym wall?

wear a temporary tattoo
of your school's mascot
on your hand

OR

on your arm

OR

on your face?

wash your basketball
team's stinky socks

OR

clean off cleats
for your entire
soccer team

OR

scrub grass stains out
of your softball team-
mates' sweats?

thank your coach with
a heartfelt card

OR

a home-cooked dinner

OR

a surprise party with
the whole team?

dress as your school
mascot at a game

OR

at a pep rally

OR

on a regular school day?

53

DREAM HOUSE

What kind of home would you love to live in?

Would you rather...

live in a home with 10 fireplaces OR 10 bathrooms OR 10 laundry rooms?

design and build your own brand-new home OR move into a historical home you admire OR choose a home you're happy with in a pretty location?

live in a city penthouse OR a mountain chalet OR a beachfront bungalow?

have an in-home elevator OR swimming pool OR sauna?

have your dream kitchen OR your dream bathroom OR your dream bedroom?

live in a perfectly styled, brand-new tiny home OR a 50-year-old ranch house OR a creepy, haunted mansion?

live in a city with 5 million people OR 100,000 people OR 500 people?

have a house with no windows OR no doors OR no roof?

live in a
farmhouse
OR
a lighthouse
OR
a hotel?

live in a camper
OR
a houseboat
OR
a railroad car?

live in the
north woods
OR
the Wild West
OR
the Far East?

live in a
medieval castle
OR
an ancient pyramid
OR
a Roman ruin?

live in the Empire
State Building
OR
the Seattle
Space Needle
OR
the White House?

live in a house
made entirely
of glass
OR
built entirely
underground
OR
built entirely
off the ground,
up in the trees?

have no plumbing
OR
no electricity
OR
no phone service?

have a backyard with
your own water slide
OR
ski slope
OR
Ferris wheel?

live in a home
once owned by
your favorite
author
OR
your favorite
movie star
OR
your favorite
athlete?

live in a small
home on a huge,
wooded lot
OR
a huge home on a
tiny lot, right next
to your neighbors
OR
a medium-size
home on a
medium-size lot?

choose your home
based on its size
OR
its style
OR
its location?

OPEN SEASON

Choose your favorite features of each time of year!

Spring

Summer

raindrops
OR
rainbows
OR
splashing in puddles?

April Fool's Day pranks
OR
Easter eggs
OR
Arbor Day trees?

spring break
OR
spring training
OR
spring cleaning?

lilies
OR
daisies
OR
roses?

baby chicks
OR
baby bunnies
OR
baby kittens?

Fourth of July picnics
OR
parades
OR
fireworks?

water balloons
OR
water slides
OR
watermelon?

count the stars
OR
catch fireflies
OR
collect seashells?

swim at the pool
OR
at the beach
OR
at the lake?

lemonade
OR
iced tea
OR
root beer?

Fall

shopping for
school supplies

OR

school clothes

OR

schoolbooks?

football games

OR

baseball
playoffs

OR

soccer practice?

hike through
fall colors

OR

hayride through
fall colors

OR

bike ride
through fall
colors?

Halloween
costumes

OR

candy

OR

haunted
houses?

pumpkin pie

OR

hot apple cider

OR

popcorn balls?

Winter

sledding

OR

skiing

OR

ice skating?

candy cane

OR

Christmas
cookie

OR

latke?

first frost

OR

first snow

OR

early thaw?

hot cocoa

OR

hot tea

OR

eggnog?

New Year's Eve

OR

Valentine's Day

OR

Groundhog Day?

POWER TRIP

In your wildest dreams, where would you travel,
and what would you do there?

Would you prefer to...

tour the world
by boat
OR
bus
OR
bicycle?

ride a zip line through
the Brazilian rain forest
OR
into the Grand Canyon
OR
down a Swiss mountainside?

camp out on a
tropical beach
OR
atop a mountain peak
OR
under a rain-forest canopy?

spend the night in a medieval
castle's dungeon
OR
in the catacombs of Paris
OR
inside a Mayan pyramid?

dine on a region's farm-fresh dishes
OR
famous gourmet meals
OR
favorite fast foods?

snack on a sweet treat
of Italian gelato
OR
French pastries
OR
Mexican churros?

walk across Europe
OR
Asia
OR
Africa?

ride a camel across the Sahara Desert
OR
a llama across the Patagonian plain
OR
an elephant through an Indian jungle?

walk on top of the
Great Wall of China

OR

walk along the Berlin Wall

OR

visit the Western Wall
in Jerusalem?

see Stonehenge in England

OR

the moai monuments on
Easter Island

OR

the abandoned city of
Machu Picchu in Peru?

stroll through a field of
lavender in the south of France

OR

a field of tulips in Holland

OR

a park filled with
cherry blossoms in Japan?

tour Buckingham
Palace in London

OR

the Palace of Versailles near Paris

OR

the Forbidden City
palace in Beijing?

bike through the Rocky Mountains

OR

across the Italian countryside

OR

along the streets of Amsterdam?

take an African safari

OR

an Alaskan whale-watching trip

OR

an Amazon River tour?

cruise through the Caribbean

OR

down the Nile River

OR

across the English Channel?

59

MAGIC MIRROR

Mirror, mirror on the wall, who's the most interesting of all?
What would you choose to see in your very own magic mirror?

Would you like to see...

your hair looking
long and lush
OR
cropped and cute
OR
a new color for
each new day?

what you'd look like
if you dressed like a
girl your age from the
1950s
OR
the 1980s
OR
the 2040s?

what your
bedroom will
look like in 10 years
OR
in 25 years
OR
in 50 years?

a conversation
taking place
between your
parents
OR
between two of
your pals
OR
between two of
your teachers?

all the
different pets
you'll ever have
OR
all the homes
you'll live in
OR
all the cars you'll
drive?

what your
favorite book
will be 10 years
from now
OR
what your
favorite movie
will be
OR
what your
favorite song
will be?

what job you will have
OR
whether you will get
married
OR
whether you will have
children?

what your mother looked like at your age

OR

what your grandmother looked like at your age

OR

what your child will look like at your age?

what your life would have been like if you lived in ancient Egypt

OR

in medieval England

OR

in the Wild West?

where you will go to college

OR

where you will live when you move away from home

OR

where you will live when you're 50 years old?

a sneak peek of your next big school test

OR

your next birthday gift

OR

your next report card?

yourself as your mother sees you

OR

as your best friend sees you

OR

as your teacher sees you?

a portrait of your family 5 years in the future

OR

a portrait that shows you with your grandchildren

OR

a portrait that shows the family of your great-great-great-great-grandchildren?

what you'd look like with bangs OR with glasses OR with braces?

SIGN ME UP!

How would you choose to lend a helping hand?

Would you rather...

volunteer at the animal shelter by feeding cats

⟪ OR ⟫

walking dogs

⟪ OR ⟫

promoting animal adoptions?

volunteer at the library by shelving books

⟪ OR ⟫

reading a story to younger kids

⟪ OR ⟫

showing senior citizens how to use the Internet?

write stories for your school newspaper

⟪ OR ⟫

take photos for your school newspaper

⟪ OR ⟫

start your own neighborhood newsletter?

visit seniors at a nursing home with your friendly pet

⟪ OR ⟫

to sing songs with your choir

⟪ OR ⟫

to help residents make a craft project?

donate food to a local food pantry

⟪ OR ⟫

stock shelves there

⟪ OR ⟫

help cook meals there?

plant a tree in a neighborhood park

⟪ OR ⟫

grow vegetables to share with a food bank

⟪ OR ⟫

grow flowers to share with your teachers?

organize your team's fund-raising bake sale

⟪ OR ⟫

bake treats to sell

⟪ OR ⟫

buy treats to eat?

write letters thanking soldiers serving abroad

 OR

collect sweet treats and snacks to send to soldiers

OR

collect games, playing cards, and movies to send to soldiers?

help build homes for people in need

OR

help build a new playground at a local park

OR

help build ramps to make spaces in your community accessible to people who use wheelchairs?

help protect the environment by biking or walking to school

OR

using less electricity at home

OR

using less water at home?

join a march for a cause you support

OR

e-mail all your friends to inform them about a cause you support

OR

write a letter to your local newspaper about a cause you support?

take charge of recycling at your home

OR

at your school

OR

at a local park?

help raise a puppy to become a service dog

OR

help care for a therapy horse

OR

help train a helper monkey?

get the chance to volunteer alongside your favorite teacher

OR

your favorite athlete

OR

your favorite movie star?

tutor younger students in math

OR

reading

OR

writing?

help needy people in your community by collecting and donating canned goods

OR

used coats and boots

OR

school supplies?

help to reduce waste by drinking from a reusable water bottle

OR

packing your lunch in washable containers

OR

starting a compost bin at home?

INGENIOUS INVENTIONS

What kinds of tricky tech do you see in your future?

Would you choose...

a car that
drives itself

washes itself

finds its own
parking spots?

a watch
that has a built-in
television

lets you know where your
friends and family are

makes sure you're never
running late?

a lunch box that
reheats your leftovers

keeps hot foods hot and cold
foods cold at the same time

refills with your
favorite snacks?

a pen that writes
perfect cursive at the
command of your voice

corrects your spelling

writes thank-you notes
and holiday cards?

a TV
that can have a
conversation with you

create shows especially for you
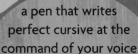
add scents to your
viewing experience?

a refrigerator that mixes special sodas made with fresh fruit
keeps your fruits and veggies fresh for months
limits how much junk food you can eat?

a hairbrush that trims your hair perfectly
changes your hair color
instantly curls or straightens your hair?

an alarm clock that tickles you awake
keeps you warm and toasty as you get up
flips you out of bed?

a hat that has built-in wireless headphones
cools your head when you get too hot
expands into an umbrella when it rains?

tennis shoes that change colors to match your outfit
make you run 50 percent faster
tie themselves?

a pet bed that brushes your kitty
a secure doggy door that opens only for your pooch
a pet translator that tells you what your furry friends are thinking?

a pop-up tent that has a built-in shower
a built-in hot tub
a built-in fireplace?

65

slippers that
warm your toes

massage your feet
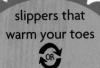
give you a pedicure?

a closet that hangs
up your clothes

folds your clothes

sews clothes that
need mending?

a shower that
dispenses shampoo
and soap

comes with a
back scrubber

instantly dries you off
without a towel?

a stove that makes
recipes automatically

cools down instantly

never burns any food?

a backpack that
floats, so you don't
feel its weight

expands to 10 times its normal size,
in case you need to carry a lot

can turn into a sleeping bag, so
you don't have to bring one on
camping trips?

a robot that
cleans
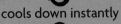
does the laundry

cooks?

a bed that makes itself

changes its own sheets

blocks light and
sound when you
are sleeping?

67

COMEDY CLUB

What do you find funny?

Are you more likely to laugh at...

a joke told by
your friend
OR
your dad or mom
OR
your teacher?

a teacher who hiccups
in front of class
OR
forgets what day it is
OR
wears crazy clothes?

a joke about animals
OR
school
OR
sports?

a video showing kids
doing pranks
OR
doing crazy dances
OR
falling into the water?

a comic strip
OR
a comic book
OR
a caricature?

a joke you make
about a friend
OR
about your family
OR
about yourself?

a squirting flower
OR
a fake spider
OR
a whoopee cushion?

videos of cats scaring dogs
OR
cats chasing laser lights
OR
cats playing piano?

a story about a kid who makes her own comic strip
OR
a kid who always gets in trouble at school
OR
a kid who always pranks her friends?

a clown who wears giant shoes
OR
an invisible dog on a leash
OR
silly magic tricks?

a silly song
OR
a limerick
OR
a poem with nonsense words?

a movie about a kid who drives a talking, flying car
OR
a kid who cannot tell a lie, no matter what
OR
a kid who magically switches bodies with her mom?

videos of babies giggling
OR
babies learning to walk
OR
babies burping?

a cartoon with a talking monkey
OR
a talking cat
OR
a talking pizza?

an app that puts silly hats on everyone in your photos
OR
puts animal ears on everyone in your photos
OR
gives everyone in your photos a crazy mustache?

a tickle from a feather
OR
a friend
OR
a kitten's whiskers?

videos of dancing dogs
OR
dogs bark-talking
OR
dogs riding motorcycles?

a knock-knock joke
OR
a pun
OR
a silly riddle?

a TV sitcom
OR
a cartoon
OR
a game show?

a book
OR
a TV show
OR
an online video?

69

WHAT'S YOUR PET PERSONALITY?

Answer these quick questions about the animals in your life.

Which pet would you prefer?

a pampered Persian cat

OR

a slinky Siamese cat

OR

a bouncy Bengal cat?

a hairless sphinx cat

OR

a wrinkly shar-pei dog

OR

a furry tarantula?

a giant Great Dane

OR

a medium cocker spaniel

OR

a tiny teacup Chihuahua?

a cat

OR

a dog

OR

a goldfish?

a trained monkey

OR

a spiky hedgehog

OR

a flying squirrel?

Would you rather...

take care of your friend's fish tank

OR

mouse house

OR

bird cages?

give a bath to a litter of pups

OR

two calm cats

OR

a single snake?

feed a giant friendly dog

OR

a grumpy cat

OR

a perky potbellied pig?

walk a puppy

OR

play with a kitten

OR

brush a bunny?

Do you like...

dogs because
they're loyal

OR

they're friendly

OR

they love
to walk?

birds because
they can fly

OR

they sing
beautifully

OR

they're good
company?

fish because
they're exotic

OR

they're relaxing
to watch

OR

they're easy to
take care of?

cats because
they purr

OR

they're fluffy

OR

they love
to play?

bunnies because
they're soft

OR

they're quiet

OR

they're cute?

horses because
they're beautiful

OR

they're powerful

OR

they're fun to
ride?

Are you more like...

a house cat

OR

a barn cat

OR

a wildcat?

a canary

OR

a cockatiel

OR

a falcon?

a poodle

OR

a greyhound

OR

a golden
retriever?

a chicken

OR

a piglet

OR

a bunny?

a mouse

OR

a ferret

OR

a guinea
pig?

an iguana

OR

a snake

OR

a chameleon?

ANIMAL ANTICS

The animal world may be more wild and crazy than you think!

Would you rather...

have a cat that could bark
OR
a dog that could purr
OR
a rabbit that could ribbit?

ride a horse with no tail
OR
a camel with no hump
OR
an elephant with
no trunk?

swim with an
underwater lion
OR
a dog with dolphin fins
OR
a web-footed wallaby?

see a squirrel
with a tiger's tail
OR
a goat with a
monkey's tail
OR
a horse with
a shark's tail?

meet a bobcat with ears
like a basset hound
OR
an elephant with
ears like a bunny
OR
a goldfish with
ears like a cat?

snuggle up inside a
kangaroo's pouch
OR
a hibernating bear's cave
OR
a robin's nest?

find a polar bear
in the rain forest
OR
a giraffe in the Arctic
OR
a camel in your backyard?

have a pet mouse
the size of a dog
OR
a pet cat the
size of a mouse
OR
a pet parakeet the
size of an eagle?

give a hippo a longer neck

OR

give a duck feet with toes

OR

give a turtle speedy legs?

have a pet fish that
could live out of water

OR

a pet mouse that could
live underwater

OR

a pet puppy that could fly?

see a carriage pulled by kangaroos

OR

a police detective
aided by an anteater

OR

an alligator that catches
mice on a farm?

hear a robin that squawks like a parrot

OR

a parrot that hisses like a snake

OR

a snake that tweets like a robin?

see a blue and orange panda

OR

a red dolphin

OR

a pink elephant?

pet a dog with no tail

OR

a cat with no whiskers

OR

a bunny with short ears?

hear a bird growl

OR

a wolf squawk

OR

a bunny howl at the moon?

see a cow with feathers

OR

a chicken with a pig's snout

OR

a pig that lays eggs?

take care of a pet
skunk with no stink

OR

a pet turtle with no shell

OR

a pet porcupine
with no quills?

spot a hummingbird
with butterfly wings

OR

a penguin with eagle's wings

OR

an ostrich with
pterodactyl wings?

73

FORTUNE COOKIE FUN

Choose how you'd fill in these fanciful fortunes.

Something you lost will soon _____.

turn up
OR
be found by a friend
OR
be forgotten

The sun always shines after _____.

nighttime
OR
a downpour
OR
an eclipse

The longest journey begins with _____.

a lot of planning
OR
a single step
OR
waiting in line at the airport

Good news will be brought to you by _____.

the one you love
OR
a mysterious stranger
OR
text message

An admirer finds you _____.

beautiful
OR
charming
OR
brilliant

The road to riches is paved with _____.

good luck
OR
$100 bills
OR
homework

Running in circles _____.

gets you nowhere
OR
makes you dizzy
OR
wears down your shoes on one side.

If you don't enjoy what you have, how could you be happier with _____?

It is better to have a hen tomorrow than _____.

a good friend
OR
a new pony
OR
more

a crowing rooster this morning
OR
a feather boa
OR
an egg today

Stop searching! Happiness is _____.

in your own heart
OR
right next to you
OR
found at home

It is better to deal with problems _____.

a distant memory
OR
your lucky day
OR
yesterday

Two days from now, tomorrow will be _____.

when your mood allows
OR
right away
OR
before they arise

75

TRADING PLACES

Imagine you could switch spots with anyone—
or anything—for just one day.

Would you rather spend a day as...

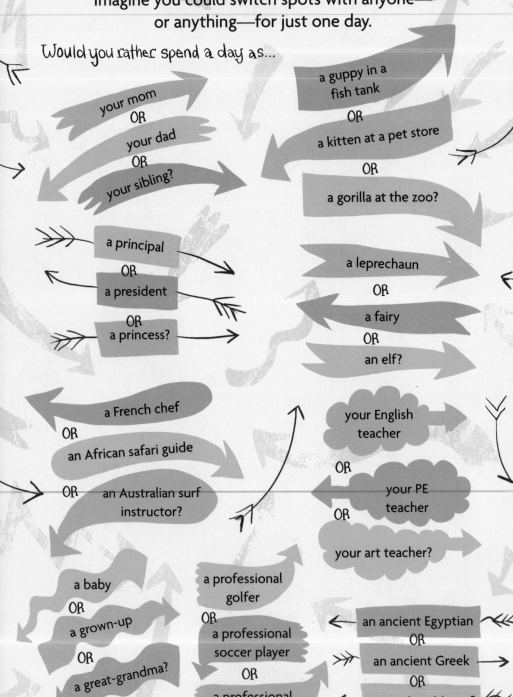

your mom
OR
your dad
OR
your sibling?

a guppy in a fish tank
OR
a kitten at a pet store
OR
a gorilla at the zoo?

a principal
OR
a president
OR
a princess?

a leprechaun
OR
a fairy
OR
an elf?

a French chef
OR
an African safari guide
OR
an Australian surf instructor?

your English teacher
OR
your PE teacher
OR
your art teacher?

a baby
OR
a grown-up
OR
a great-grandma?

a professional golfer
OR
a professional soccer player
OR
a professional tennis player?

an ancient Egyptian
OR
an ancient Greek
OR
an ancient Mayan?

a novelist

OR

a painter

OR

a poet?

an attorney

OR

a judge

OR

a member of a jury?

an oak tree
in a city park

OR

a giant redwood
in a tall forest

OR

a spruce on a
Christmas
tree farm?

a poodle

OR

a golden retriever

OR

a bulldog?

an Olympic gold
medalist

OR

a Nobel Prize winner

OR

an Academy
Award winner?

a police detective

OR

a private investigator

OR

a master thief?

a chicken

OR

an egg

OR

an omelet?

your favorite musician

OR

your favorite actor

OR

your favorite athlete?

Frosty the Snowman

OR

the Abominable Snowman

OR

Jack Frost?

your best friend

OR

your biggest enemy

OR

your hero?

EMOJI ANSWERS

Choose an emoji to post your response to each situation below!

snow day

getting grounded

broken arm

summer camp

getting glasses

visiting a new country

late for school

a surprise party

straight As on your report card

first time in New York City

favorite restaurant

going camping

homework you can't figure out

best friend's birthday

pepperoni pizza

new pet

going to a horror movie

getting braces

going to a baseball game

Halloween party

beach vacation

moving to a new house

school lunch

last day of school

Which This or That . . . or That? questions were your favorites?
Create your own and send them to:

Editor, *This or That . . . or That? Quiz Book*
American Girl
8400 Fairway Place
Middleton, WI 53562

Here are some other American Girl®
books you might like.

Each sold separately. Find more books online at americangirl.com.

Parents, request a FREE catalog at **americangirl.com/catalog**.
Sign up at **americangirl.com/email** to receive the latest news and exclusive offers.

Discover online games, quizzes, activities,
and more at **americangirl.com/play**